RIADH MONIR

A polyglottic Algeria

A polyphonic press

RIADH MONIR

A polyglottic Algeria
A polyphonic press

ScienciaScripts

Imprint

Any brand names and product names mentioned in this book are subject to trademark, brand or patent protection and are trademarks or registered trademarks of their respective holders. The use of brand names, product names, common names, trade names, product descriptions etc. even without a particular marking in this work is in no way to be construed to mean that such names may be regarded as unrestricted in respect of trademark and brand protection legislation and could thus be used by anyone.

Cover image: www.ingimage.com

This book is a translation from the original published under ISBN 978-620-7-48009-8.

Publisher:
Sciencia Scripts
is a trademark of
Dodo Books Indian Ocean Ltd. and OmniScriptum S.R.L publishing group

120 High Road, East Finchley, London, N2 9ED, United Kingdom
Str. Armeneasca 28/1, office 1, Chisinau MD-2012, Republic of Moldova, Europe
Printed at: see last page
ISBN: 978-620-3-56635-2

Polyglottic Algeria

A polyphonic press

Thank you

I'd like to thank all the members of my family, my parents and brothers, and especially Karim.

I would like to thank Ms Mazot Aouda, Mr Rolf Kailuweit and Mr Fernand Hörner.

I'd also like to thank the people who encouraged me to do this work.

Table of contents

Introduction

This work is a summary of the linguistic situation in Algeria and the polyphonic state of the Algerian written press, given that the Algerian territory is rich in spoken languages such as Arabic, French, Spanish etc... there is a linguistic diversity, which generates a polyphony within the Algerian journalistic statement, which includes the different languages spoken in Algeria. Knowing that polyphony, according to Ducrot (1980), is the plurality of voices within an utterance, we can pose the following central question: how does linguistic diversity in Algeria engender a polyphonic situation within the Algerian journalistic utterance? A number of postulates follow from this questioning:

- the diversity of discourse in different languages generates polyphonic journalistic statements.

The methodology followed in this work is the localization of marks of linguistic diversity within Algerian journalistic utterances and the functional critique of these identified marks.

The aim of this work is the polyphonic study of the marks of linguistic diversity resulting from local Algerian speech, in other words the aim is the polyphonic study of the lexemes resulting from the linguistic diversity existing within the Algerian territory.

This work is divided into two chapters, the first of which summarizes the linguistic situation in Algeria and the linguistic diversity that exists there. The second chapter deals with the polyphonic study of Algerian journalistic utterances.

The first chapter deals with the different languages spoken in Algeria, such as Arabic, French, Berber, Spanish, etc. In this chapter, we have drawn on the work of Monir (2023) and Taleb Ibrahimi (2004) to address the notions of Arabic, Berber, French, Spanish, Algerian dialect and English in Algeria.

The second chapter deals with the polyphonic study of different forms of linguistic diversity such as: codic alternation, neology etc... we have drawn on the theoretical basis of Ducrot (1980) and Nølke (2017).

Language situation in Algeria

Arabic

Arabic is one of the Semitic languages spoken in Algeria. Standard Arabic, Classical Arabic or Fosha[1] is considered an official language, as Monir (2023) points out: "The Arabic language, as a standard language or Fosha17, covers the whole territory, including other countries such as Tunisia, Morocco, Mauritania, Egypt, Qatar, Saudi Arabia... etc.". In addition, it should be noted that Classical Arabic is the first official language of the Algerian state, used in administration, the media and education". (2023 :85). Although this language is spoken in the majority of the Arab world, as in Egypt and Qatar, it has a sub-variety used in Algeria, namely the Algerian dialect, which we will discuss in the next section.

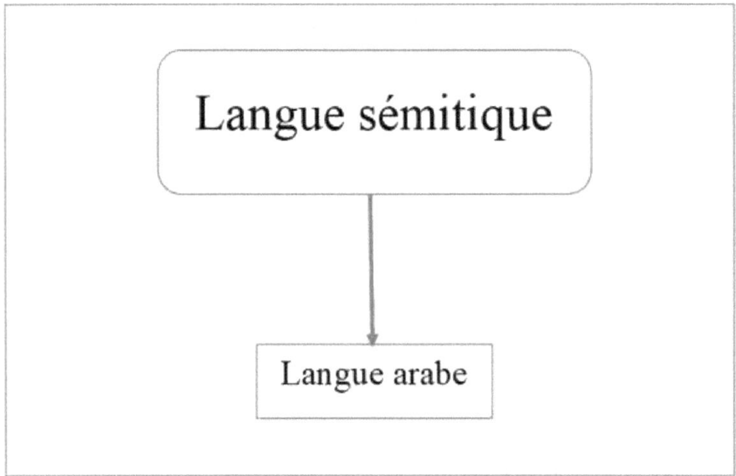

Arabic is used in Algeria through the Islamic futuhats[2] , through which Arab Muslims wanted to spread Islam[3] around the world, the Arabic language is the means for the growth of the Islamic religion

---

[1] Classical Arabic.
[2] Conquests to spread the Islamic religion.
[3] A religion whose aim is the absolute worship of Allah and the propagation of peace in the world.

because the Koran[4] , the shariaa[5] and the sunna[6] are in Arabic (but can be translated except the Koran we can only translate its tafsir[7]).

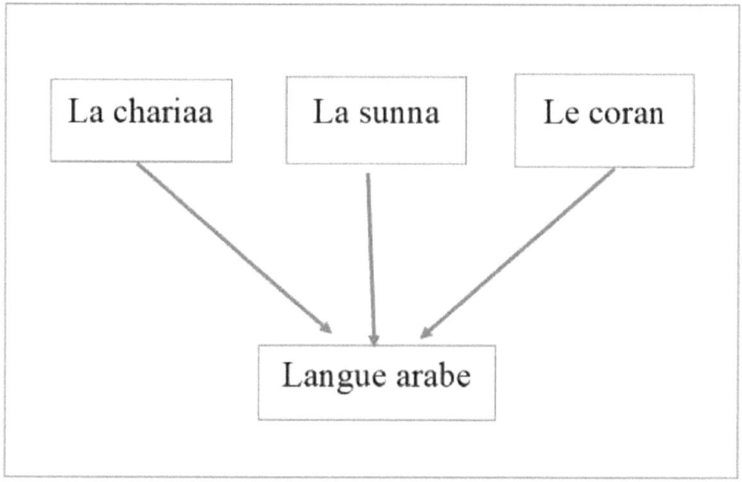

The Arabic language is used throughout Algeria, in administration, schools and the media. Each of Algeria's[8] wilayas has its own radio station broadcasting in Arabic.

---

[4] Sacred book containing the word of Allah.
[5] The principles of Islam.
[6] The lifestyle and spirituality of the Prophet Muhammad, peace and blessings be upon him.
[7] A book explaining the true meaning of Koranic verses.
[8] One of the states making up the Algerian state.

French

According to Monir (2023): "Franco-Algerian cohabitation, which lasted 132 years, gave rise to spontaneous use of the French language without eliminating the primordial language, Arabic, which means that alongside local Algerian speech, French is always used, because of the acquisition of this language during the French occupation of Algeria." (2023 : 94). French came to Algeria through the French military occupation of Algeria, which lasted 132 years. The French occupation forced Algerians to use French in administration, at school and in the Algerian media landscape. According to Monir (2023): "After the liberation of Oranese soil from Spanish occupation, another military occupation was established, that of the French, for the entire Algerian territory, and the French language was imposed on the Algerian people in their daily lives and taught in schools, an attempt was made to suppress the Arabic language, except that the Algerian people attended the mosque at least five times a day; this religious institution protected the Arabic language from suppression by giving them the opportunity to recite the Koran, which is the sacred book of Islam given by Allah, written in Arabic." (2023 : 94).

On the other hand, there was a certain resistance to the Arabic language in Algerian territory during the French occupation, as the use of Arabic for prayer and recitation of the Koran was maintained in mosques and zaouias[9] and the principles of the Arabic language were even taught there, in order to preserve the Arab-Algerian identity and to keep Islam as a religion and an identity belonging, in order not to submit to the whims of the occupiers, which are to suppress the Arabic language by replacing it with French, to suppress the Islamic religion by replacing it with Christianity, and to eliminate the Arab-Algerian identity by replacing it with French naturalization. Taleb Ibrahimi (2004) asserts that: "French, the language imposed on the Algerian people by fire and blood, was one of the fundamental elements used by colonial power to perfect its hold on the conquered country and accelerate the enterprise of destructuring, depersonalizing and

---

[9] Koranic school.

acculturating a territory that had become an integral part of the 'mother country', France." (2004 : 210).

Today, French is widely used in Algeria, according to Taleb Ibrahimi (2004): "It was after 1962 that the use of French spread. The immense educational efforts made by the young state (with the cooperation of the former colonizer) easily explain the expansion of the use of the French language, which by necessity became the language of administration, with the proportion of literates in this language far exceeding that of literates in Arabic." (2004 : 211). French is present in the administration (for example, when extracting civil status papers, it is possible to have them in French), it is present at school, as French is taught as a fundamental subject to pupils at different levels (primary, middle and secondary),

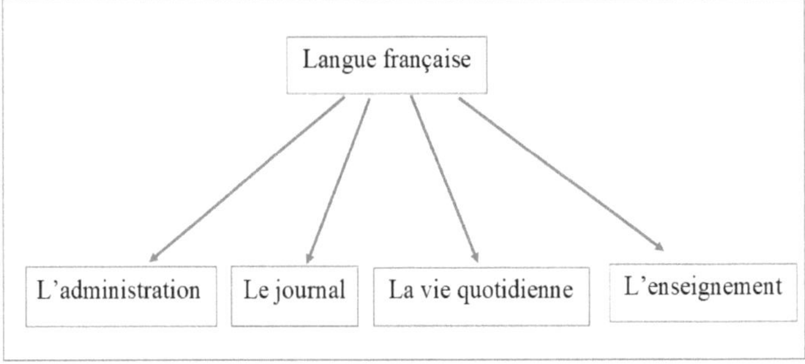

Taleb Ibrahimi (2004) considers that: "Until 1978, when the fully Arabized Basic School was introduced, the school system was characterized by linguistic duality. For one-third of classes, teaching was entirely in Arabic, while for the remaining two-thirds, Arabic was used for literary subjects and French for scientific subjects. After this date, French was only taught from the third year of primary school onwards, and a little later from the fourth year. Secondary education was fully Arabicized by the end of the 1988-1989 school year. The teaching of French as a foreign language largely declined, and even virtually disappeared in certain regions of the interior and south. However, there was still a significant gap between Arabic-language secondary education and higher education, where French remained the language of instruction in many scientific fields. Students need to be brought up to the same level, and there is a huge drop-out rate, with a particularly high repetition rate. In an attempt to remedy this situation, the authorities have launched a vast program to rehabilitate the teaching of French, as well as other foreign languages, as part of the reform of the Algerian school system initiated in the early 2000s". (2004 : 211). French is also present in the press in all its forms, as confirmed by Monir (2023): "Today, French is still taught in educational institutions. However, the French language is also used in the written media" (2023: 95).

Berber

Berber is Algeria's second official language, after Arabic. The Berber language is used in Morocco, Tunisia and even Egypt, because before the French military occupation, there were no borders between Morocco, Algeria and Tunisia; there was a single territory that was home to all three peoples, and which is called *the North African Star*, as Monir (2023) points out: "Before the Islamic opening up (*futuhat al islamiya*), present-day Algeria was home to the Tuaregs, the Beni-Zabs and the Berber Kabyle. These tribes shared a single language, which is Berber; it's essential to remember that Morocco and Tunisia also share the same Berber language, because before the French occupation of North Africa (Morocco, Algeria and Tunisia) there were no borders" (2023: 88).

Berber is a language that is subdivided into several language sub-varieties, which are scattered throughout the Algerian territory. According to Taleb Ibrahimi (2004), there are several sub-varieties of Berber: "Kabyle or Taqbaylit (Kabylie), Chaoui or Tachaouit (Aurès), Mzabi (Mzab) and Targui or Tamachek of the Tuaregs of the deep south (Hoggar and Tassili)". (2004 :208). *Taqbaylit* is used in Greater Kabylia (Tizi-Ouzou) and Lesser Kabylia (Bejaia), while *Chaoui* is used in the Aures region of Algeria (Batna); *Mzabi* is another sub-variety of Berber, spoken in southern Algeria (Ghardaïa); and finally, there's *Targui*, spoken in Algeria's deep south (Hoggar and Tassili).

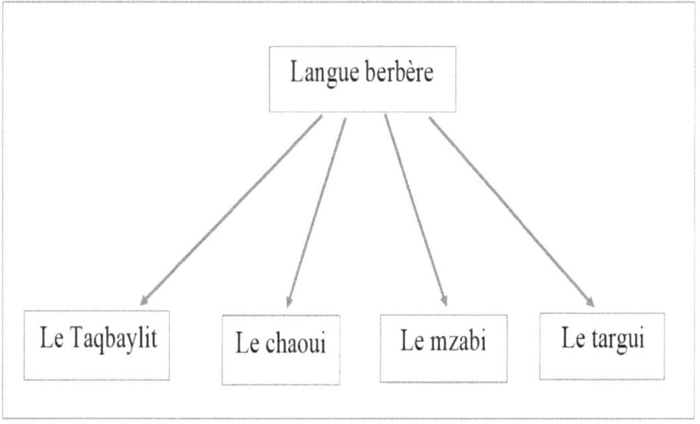

Today, Berber is taught in schools as a fundamental subject and at universities as part of the university curriculum. Berber has a prominent place in Algeria's media landscape, with a radio station dedicated to Berber-language radio programs, and Berber-language TV channels such as *Berbère Tv*. Finally, there are a dozen newspapers, published daily, weekly and fortnightly, which broadcast in Berber in a regulated, organized and excessive manner.

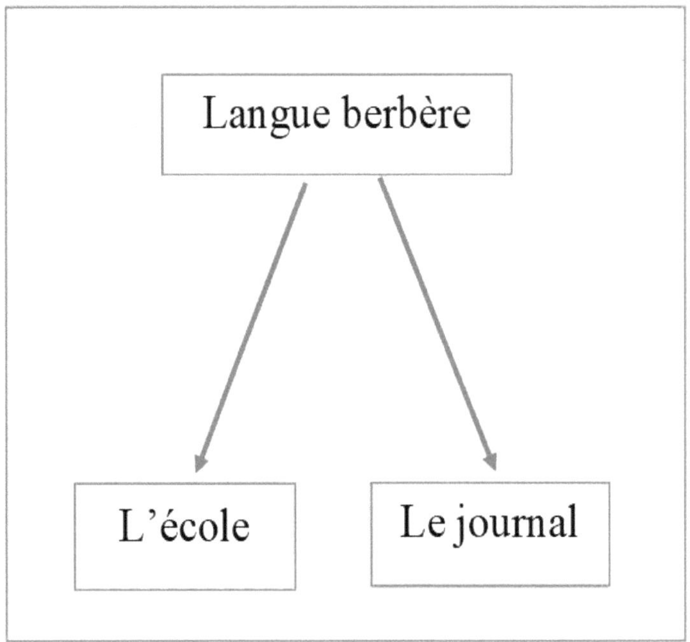

Spanish

Spanish, being one of the Latin languages, came to Algeria through the Spanish military occupation, and when the Spanish occupied the city of Oran as a territory belonging to Spain, there was a cohabitation of the Spanish people with the Algerian people of Oran. According to Taleb Ibrahimi (2004): "before the arrival of the Ottomans, Algerians had also been in contact with European languages. This was notably the case with Spanish in the west of the country, primarily due to the Spanish colonial presence for three centuries in the city of Oran". (2004 :210)

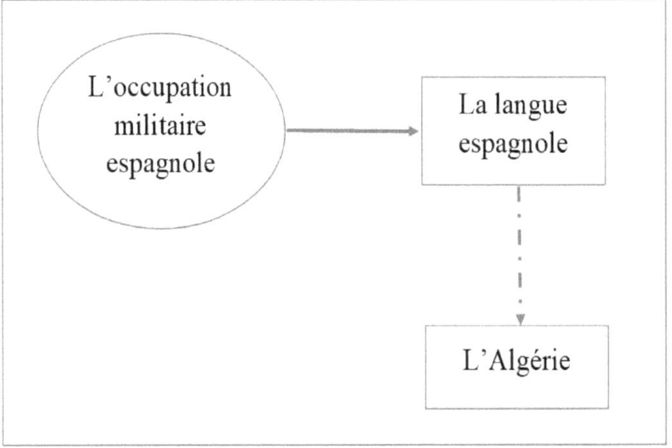

Monir (2023) attests that: "A whole new culture was established on Oranese soil, such as: gastronomy, churches and elsewhere the Santa Cruz church is the best living example, which never ceases to attest to the presence of Spanish culture in Oran...etc." (2023: 90). Spain built certain buildings, such as the Santa Cruz Cathedral, which today is the symbol and concrete proof of the Spanish presence in Oran. There were neighborhoods with Spanish names, such as Santiago.

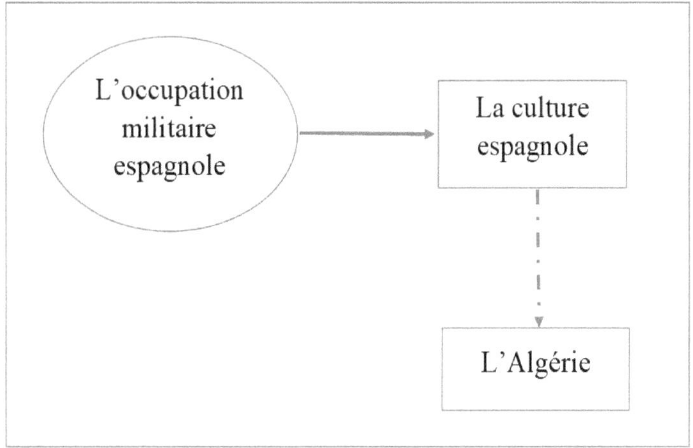

During the Spanish-Oranian cohabitation, Spanish terms were borrowed into everyday Algerian speech, as Monir (2023) shows: "The Spaniards shared the city of Oran with the real Oranese natives, so they cohabited in the same city and shared the same daily life, these Oranese natives acquired little Spanish lexicon, and this acquisition was inculcated in the Oranese from generation to generation." (2023 : 91). In addition, certain Spanish culinary recipes were borrowed, such as paella and Spanish-style peppers and Carane[10]

Today, Spanish is used in the Oran region, in everyday conversations Spanish terms are used in the speech chain, which is certainly in Algerian dialect. Spanish is present in Algeria in general, and in Oran in particular, and is taught in high schools, universities, language learning centers and the Cervantes Center.

---

[10] Chickpea gratin.

English

In the face of the immense changes taking place in the world today, thanks to advances in knowledge and technology, almost all research is carried out in the English language. Despite this, the world has undergone a violent wave of anglicism.

English is indispensable for interpersonal communication on an international scale, and is used in major commercial exchanges all over the world. Etc...

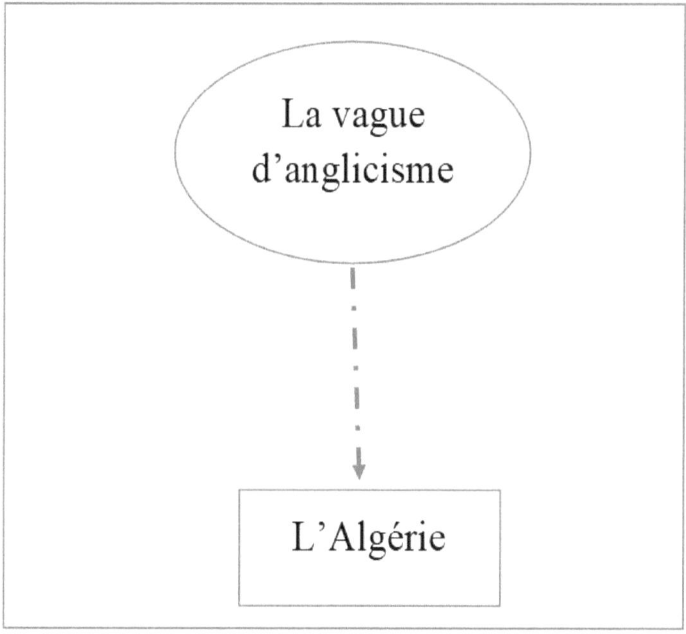

Algeria is one of the countries in the world that has suffered this wave of Anglicism, and today the higher education and scientific research sector has introduced the English language into courses at Algerian universities. English is also being introduced in primary classes (from the second year). Young Algerians are learning English thanks to American films and songs. English is also present in the Algerian press, as on the Algerian TV channel *Algérie 24*. In Algerian society, English terms are used in local speech to designate a specific meaning.

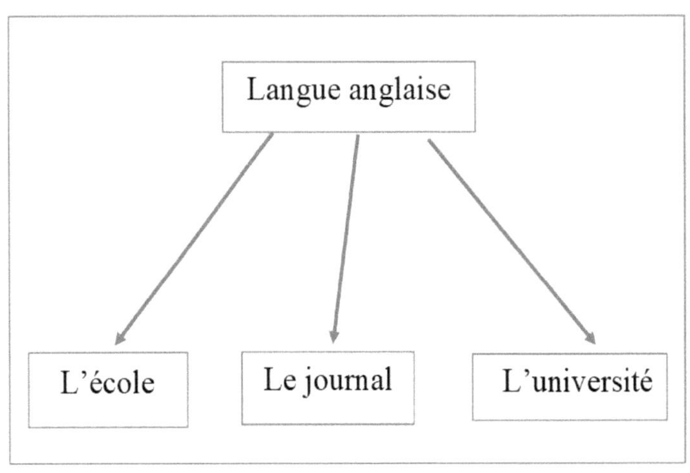

Langue anglaise
L'école
Le journal
L'université

The Algerian dialect

The Algerian dialect is a mixture of ancient and modern languages, according to Taleb Ibrahimi (2004): "the register whose acquisition and use are the most spontaneous, what we commonly call dialects or parlers" (2004: 207). The Algerian dialect is made up of the ancient Punic language, classical Arabic, French, Turkish, Berber, Spanish and English. The Algerian dialect is rich in lexicon, borrowing lexemes and expressions from several languages to communicate in everyday life.

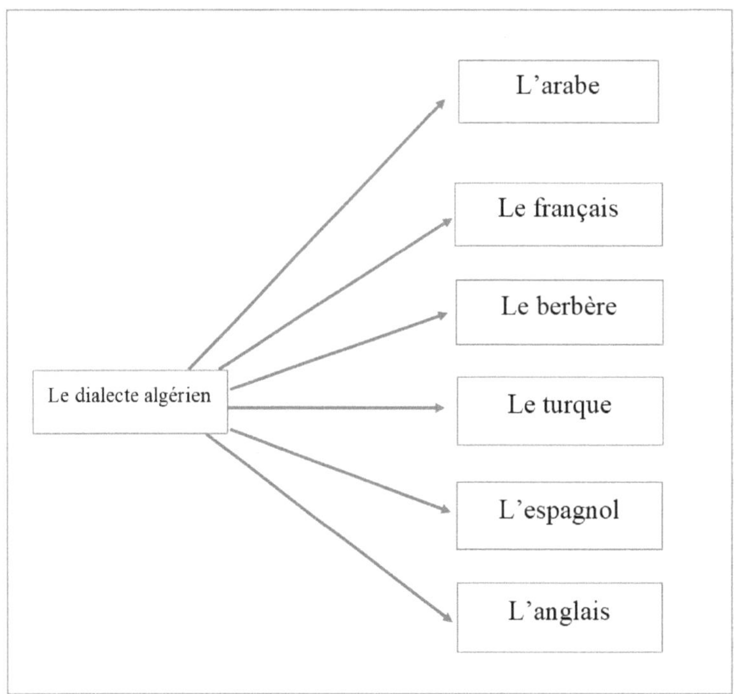

According to Monir (2023): "Regional languages are part of the Algerian dialect, i.e., the sum total of all languages is the Algerian dialect. In other words, there is a linguistic consciousness in Algeria that encompasses all dialects" (2023:86), bearing in mind that the Algerian territory is vast, with several regions and wilayas, and that each wilaya is made up of several towns and cities, the Algerian dialect covers the entire Algerian territory. On the other hand, there is a fluctuation in Algerian dialect across the different Algerian regions.

According to Taleb Ibrahimi (*ibid.*): "four main dialect regions: the East around Constantine, the Algérois and its hinterland, the Oranie and then the South, from the Saharan Atlas" (2004: 207). The western dialect, *Lahdjat el Gharb*, is used in the Oranie region (all the wilayas around Oran), and is more or less identical to the local Moroccan dialect. There's the eastern Algerian dialect *Lahdjat echark*, used in the Annaba region and the surrounding wilayas to the east, which is more or less similar to the local Tunisian dialect. Then there's the Algerian dialect, used in the Algiers region (all the wilayas surrounding Algiers). This dialect has no similar speakers.

Finally, there's the Southern Algerian dialect, used in the south and far south of Algeria. This dialect is roughly identical to the local Mauritanian language.

There's a difference between the different kinds of Algerian dialects, both semantically and in terms of pronunciation: each region has its own pronunciation and its own semantic value to the same common Algerian lexemes. Algeria is rich in languages that are used in the same territory and that fit into different local dialects.

Algerian polyglossy and linguistic polyphony in Algeria

Corpus :

The corpus collected (in the appendices) for this study is derived from three Algerian newspapers: *El Watan, L'Echo d'Algérie* and *Liberté*. These are general-interest papers published daily, with an average circulation of 12,000 copies per day. All three are written in French, and sell in Algeria as well as in France.

Polyphony :

Polyphony is originally a musical concept, the assembly of the sounds of several instruments to create harmonious music. The harmony of sounds and the cooperation that exists between the sounds of different musical instruments lead to a final product that is coherent music.

Linguistic polyphony :

Polyphony also exists in linguistics, which is, according to Ducrot (1980): "when one interprets an utterance, to hear expressed in it *a plurality of voices* different from that of the speaker, or as some grammarians say about Words that the speaker does not take into account, but puts, explicitly or not, between quotation marks, a 'polyphony'". (1980 : 44). Polyphony is the multitude of voices that exist within an utterance, knowing that this multitude of voices is quite different from the speaker's voice.

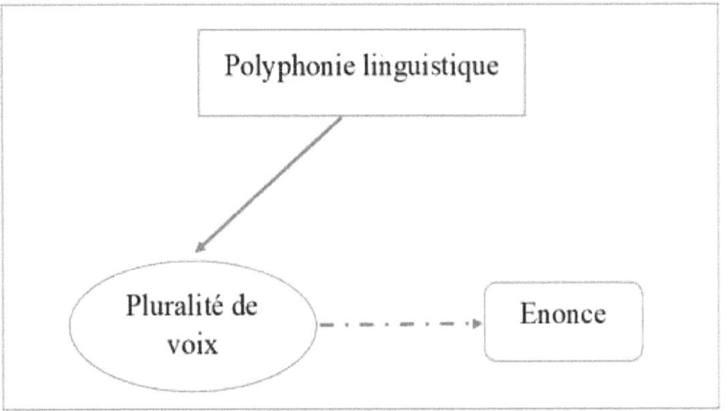

For further clarification, Ducrot (1984) reaffirms that: "for Bakhtin, there is a whole category of texts, and in particular literary texts, for which it is necessary to know that several voices speak simultaneously.

texts, for which it is necessary to know that several voices speak simultaneously,

without one of them being preponderant and judging the others". (1984 : 171). Polyphony is the phenomenon of a variety of voices existing within an utterance, while emphasizing the characteristic that each of the voices is free in relation to the others, and that one of the voices can hardly judge the other.

Polyphony, on the other hand, is different, according to Nølke (2017): "it is widely recognized that in most cases texts communicate many different points of view attributable to various speech participants. The normal situation is that two or more voices are heard in the same text; texts are polyphonic" (2017: 36). Linguistic polyphony is little different according to Nølke, it is a diversity of viewpoints that exists within a given utterance, this diversity of viewpoints is governed by a certain harmony.

What's more, we can't talk about linguistic polyphony without addressing the concept of dialogism, the driving force behind it.

Dialogism :

Dialogism comes from dialogue, which is the opposite of monologue, according to Bakhtin (1979/1984): "The expression of an utterance is always, in varying degrees, a response, in other words: it manifests not only its own relationship to the object of the utterance, but also the speaker's relationship to the utterances of others. The forms of reaction-response that fill an utterance are extraordinarily varied and, until now, have never been studied" (1979/1984: 299). Dialogism is a reaction that takes the form of a question/answer within an utterance; the question is always hidden, but the answer is always more or less clear, and this answer is generated by the speaker. Bakhtin (1984) confirms that: "Responsive understanding of a verbal whole is always dialogic." (1984 :336-337). Dialogism is attached to the interactive response, which presents itself as a voice that could polyphonize a given utterance.

The text island :

The îlot textuel is a form of reported discourse par excellence, from which a number of properties result, which we'll detail below. According to Authier-Revuz (2020), the textual islet is: "academic presentations centered on enunciation - textuality, narration - which, if they mention, alongside the "classic" forms of DR - variously articulated with these and under varied appellations : connotation autonymique, mise entre guillemets, îlots textuels, ... - forms which, in terms of ways of saying, do indeed come under the heading of modalisation autonymique d'emprunt (MAE), modalisation par discours autre (MDA), do not mention the sector, so rich and so present in discourse, of MAS22 " (2020: 81). The textual island is DR the reported discourse, whatever its nature; it is placed in brackets to signal the authentication of the statement, which comes from a given enunciator.

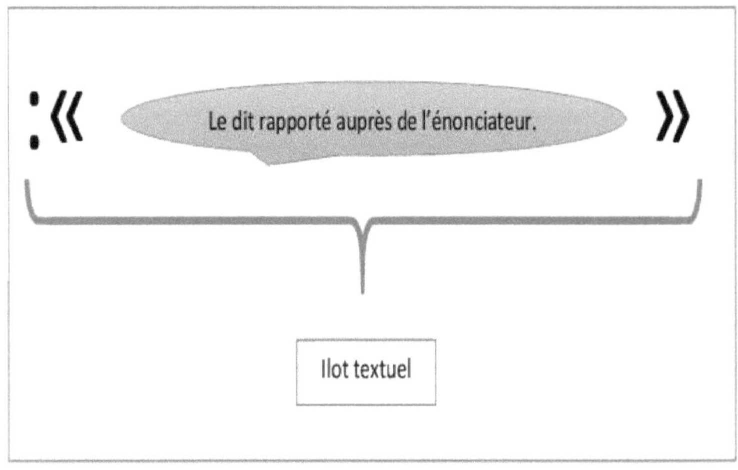

The textual island gives rise to modalizations, including :

- (MAE) autonymic borrowing modalization :

It guarantees that the reported utterance is taken up again; according to the name of this modalization, it is a total borrowing of the reported utterance from a speaker.

- (MDA) speech modalization other :

It appears as marks within the utterance reported to the speaker, showing that this utterance is original and is the cognate of the same speaker. These marks can be expressions of emotion or opinion, or even personal pronouns.

- (RDA) other speech representation :

These marks show that the discourse is not the property of the speaker, but of the speaker who uttered it in the first place.

Authier-Revuz (2020) also adds that the phenomenon of the textual island: "designates *one* of the configurations of the appearance of the MAE, in the context of the GDR," (2020: 303). The textual islet *"Azul Fellawen, thanmirthenwen imi dussaem gherghouri (thank you for coming to see me tonight", the singer will say,* is a discourse reported by the journalist-locuteur to the readership, this fragment is enunciated in Berber and in French, this fragment is part of the Algerian journalistic statement entitled *Soirées du Ramadhan: La chanteuse kabyle, Yasmina, subjugate son public à Bouira*. The fragment is enclosed in quotation marks and retains its Berber and French transcription for the purpose of preserving the originality of the textual islet; quotation marks are the autonymic modality of borrowing, the act of borrowing an utterance from its true author or enunciator. *Azul Fellawen, thanmirthenwen imi dussaem gherghouri (thank you for coming to see me tonight)* is not specific to the journalist-speaker, but is the utterance of an enunciator who is a singer. According to the decomposition of the textual islet, there is a first voice, that of the singer, which appears in the textual islet *"Azul Fellawen, thanmirthenwen imi dussaem gherghouri (thank you for coming to see me tonight)"*. On the other hand, the support for this textual island is the rest of the Algerian journalistic statement entitled *Soirées du Ramadhan: La chanteuse kabyle, Yasmina, subjugate son public à Bouira*, which represents the voice of the journalist-locuteur. The Algerian journalistic statement *Soirées du Ramadhan: La chanteuse kabyle, Yasmina, subjugue son public à Bouira* is polyphonic in that it comprises two voices, the first that of the enunciator (the singer) and the second that of the journalist-locuteur.

Codic alternation :

The phenomenon of code alternation is the contact of two different codes within a single utterance, where there is grammatical and syntactic concordance, ensuring lucid meaning. According to Gumperz (1989): "The juxtaposition within the same verbal exchange of passages where the discourse belongs to two different grammatical systems or subsystems. Most often, alternation takes the form of two consecutive sentences. As when a speaker uses a second language either to reiterate his message or to respond to someone else's assertion". (1989 : 57). Codic alternation is the juxtaposition of two codes, which are two different languages, within an utterance, knowing that these two codes have completely different grammatical systems, but which achieve a certain harmony within the utterance to convey a meaning.

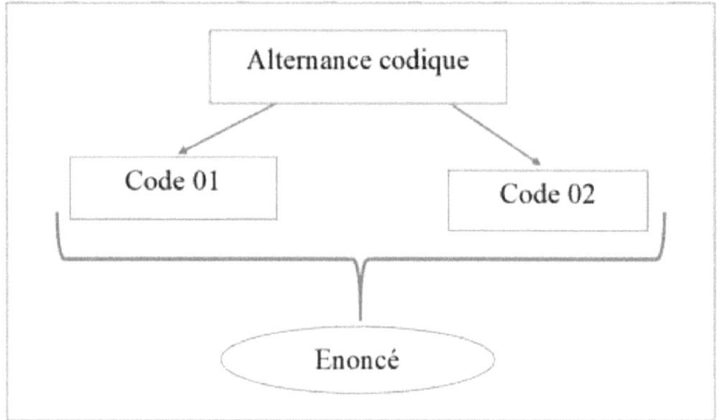

The codic alternation mark *"Ulac smah ulac", "Azul fellawen", "Tubiret d-Imazighen"*, which we have identified in our corpus, has its origins in the Berber language, which has its own lexical structure and grammatical system based on Berber grammar, on the other hand, there is a certain harmony between the codic alternation mark *"Ulac smah ulac", "Azul fellawen", "Tubiret d-Imazighen"* and the body of the journalistic text in French. The speaker, who employs the phenomenon of codic alternation within another text body in another language, creates and weaves a certain linguistic link between the two text bodies, which brings the two lexical and grammatical systems into a certain coordination, creating harmony between the two bodies. In linguistic polyphony, each body represents a polyphonic voice, so *"Ulac smah ulac", "Azul fellawen", "Tubiret d-Imazighen"* represents a polyphonic voice in its own right within the Algerian journalistic utterance, which in turn represents another polyphonic voice. Furthermore, the codic alternation mark *"Ulac smah ulac", "Azul fellawen", "Tubiret d-Imazighen"* derives from the enunciator-demonstrators, revealing that the latter is their own voice, while the body of the Algerian journalistic utterance contanat the codic alternation mark is the apparent of the journalist-speaker, making the latter a second voice. Two voices (the codic alternation mark *"Ulac smah ulac", "Azul fellawen", "Tubiret d-*

Imazighen" and the whole body of the Algerian journalistic statement including the codic alternation mark) within a single statement reveals that this Algerian journalistic statement entitled *Le MAK et le MCB dans le calme* is polyphonic.

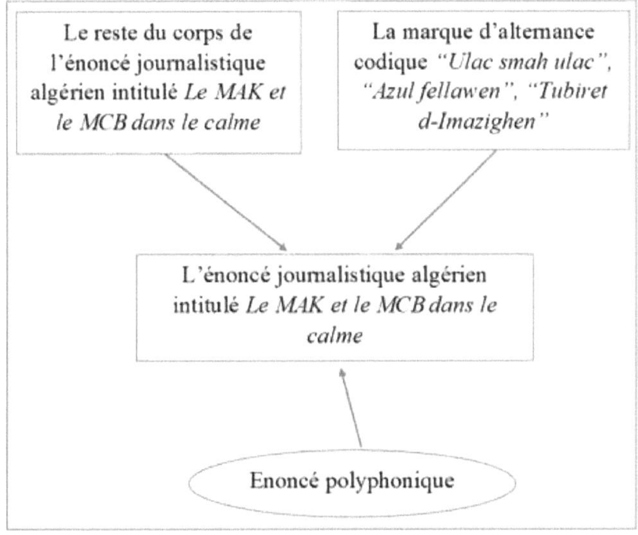

The codic alternation mark *"Ntouma kbah w hna samtine w samet yarleb lekbih"* is juxtaposed with the body of the Algerian journalistic statement entitled *8th Friday of protest in Oran: A spectacular mobilization and flawless discipline!* Where there is a certain harmony between the two languages' grammatical systems, despite their divergence.

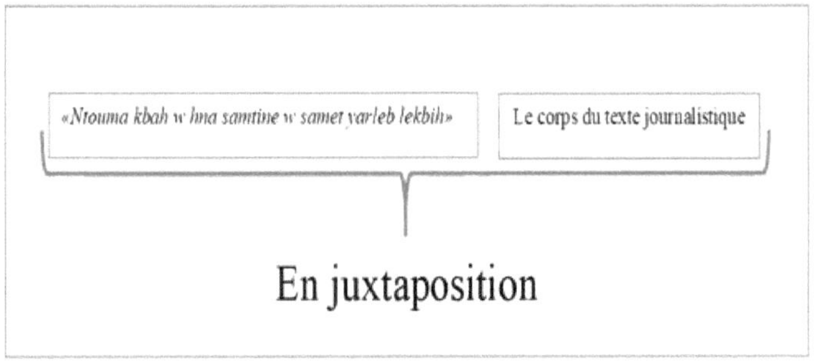

The codic alternation mark *"Ntouma kbah w hna samtine w samet yarleb lekbih"* is presented as an utterance proper to the enunciator-demonstrators, the rest of the body of the Algerian journalistic utterance entitled *8th Friday protest in Oran: Spectacular mobilization and unfailing discipline!* represents the utterance of the journalist-locutor. The enunciator-demonstrators expressed their polyphonic voice with the statement *"Ntouma kbah w hna samtine w samet yarleb lekbih",* the journalist-locuteur presents his voice under the rest of the body of the Algerian journalistic statement entitled *8th Friday of protest in Oran: A spectacular mobilization and unfailing discipline!* Two voices within a single utterance produces a polyphonic utterance. The Algerian journalistic utterance *8th Friday of protest in Oran: A spectacular mobilization and unfailing discipline!* includes the voice of the journalist-locuteur and the voice of the enunciator-demonstrators, so this Algerian journalistic utterance is polyphonic.

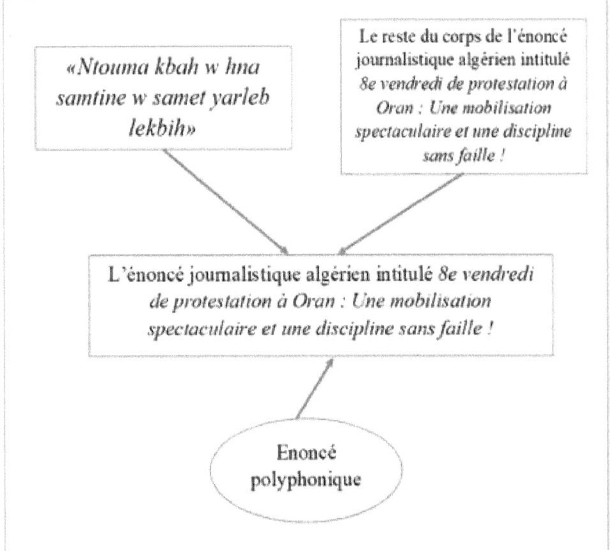

Lexical borrowing :

The phenomenon of lexical borrowing is frequently present in the written press, to cover the semantic needs of the journalistic statement.

According to Dubois (1994), borrowing is: "a linguistic unit or feature that previously existed in a language B (called the source language) and that A did not possess, [used and integrated into] a language A" (1994: 177). Borrowing is the use of a lexeme from a language called 01 in another language called 02. This process involves adaptation and insertion into the lending language; for the borrowed lexeme to be adequately harmonic in language 02, certain lexical and grammatical conditions must be met. Because, according to Bres (2005), borrowing is: "a set of extremely heterogeneous linguistic marks" (2005: 12). The heterogeneity that exists in the phenomenon of borrowing calls for grammatical and lexical adaptation so that the utterance comprising the borrowing is legible and endowed with clear meaning.

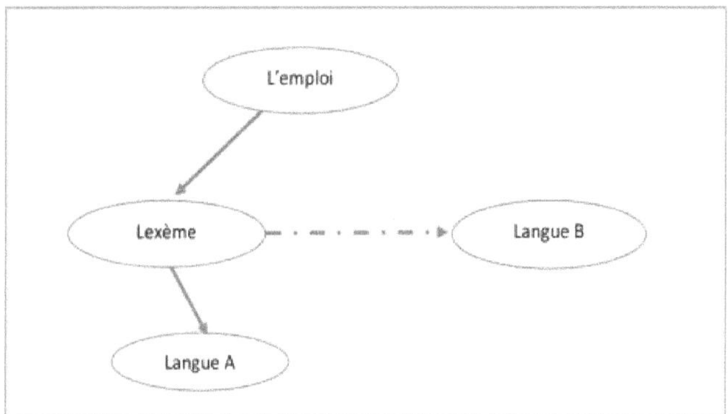

The lexical borrowing mark "*Hibra ala ouarak*" is in perfect harmony with the text of the Algerian journalistic statement entitled *Reappropriation of the Algerian revolution and/or independence*, as the borrowing mark "*Hibra ala ouarak*" has taken the same grammatical and lexical form as the body of the text of the Algerian journalistic statement *Reappropriation of the Algerian revolution and/or independence*. Of course, when we borrow a lexeme from another language, it has to be more or less compatible with the grammatical system of the borrowing language. In linguistic polyphony, the borrowing mark "*Hibra ala ouarak*" represents a voice that is specific to a given enunciator, who first generated the borrowing mark "*Hibra*

ala ouarak" as a borrowing phenomenon. On the other hand, the rest of the body text of the Algerian journalistic statement entitled *Reappropriation of the Algerian Revolution and/or Independence* represents the second voice that refers back to the journalist-speaker. So, within the Algerian journalistic statement entitled *Reappropriation of the Algerian revolution and/or independence,* there are two completely different and independent voices (one does not depend on the other), which means that this Algerian journalistic statement is polyphonic.

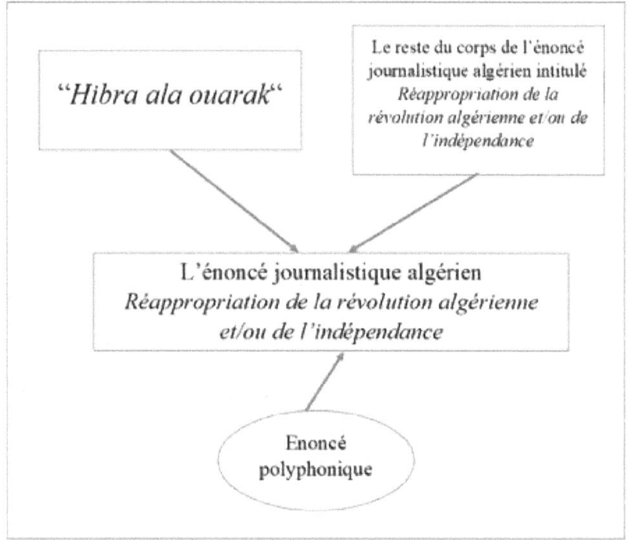

The borrowing mark *itnahaou Gaâ* is one of the voices present in the Algerian journalistic statement entitled *Reappropriation of the Algerian Revolution and/or Independence*. This voice is derived from a given enunciator, who has enunciated *itnahaou Gaâ* and for which he assumes enunciative responsibility. In contrast, the body of text of the Algerian journalistic statement entitled *Reappropriation of the Algerian Revolution and/or Independence,* which includes the borrowing mark, is the voice of the journalist-locuteur, whose enunciative responsibility is imputed to the latter. Within the Algerian journalistic statement entitled *Reappropriation of the Algerian revolution and/or*

independence there is a plurality of voices: one is proper to the journalist-locuteur and the other is the product of a given enunciator, which concludes that the Algerian journalistic statement entitled *Reappropriation of the Algerian revolution and/or independence* is polyphonic.

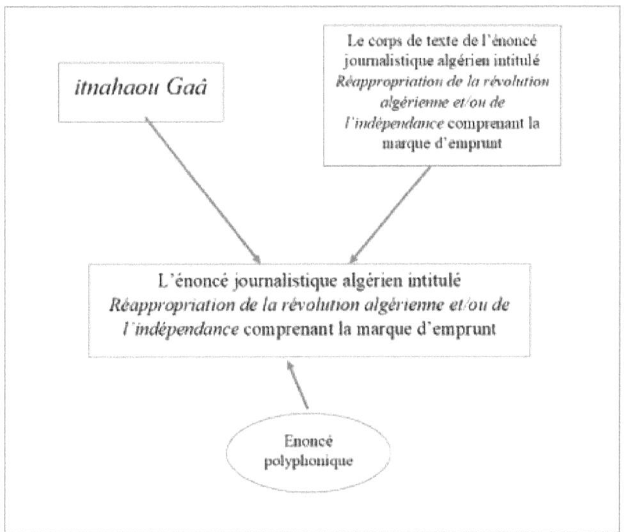

Neology :

The phenomenon of neology is the creation of a term for lexical purposes. According to Guilbert (1973) neology: "is a linguistic sign with a 'signifier' side and a 'signified' side. These two components are jointly modified in neological creation, even if the mutation seems to concern only the morphology of the term or only its meaning." (1973 : 18). Neology is the creation of a signifier and a signified, to meet the needs of a language lacking certain lexemes. Neology is always subject to the grammatical norms of the creating language; we must always follow the grammatical structure of the creating language in order to create a suitable new lexeme.

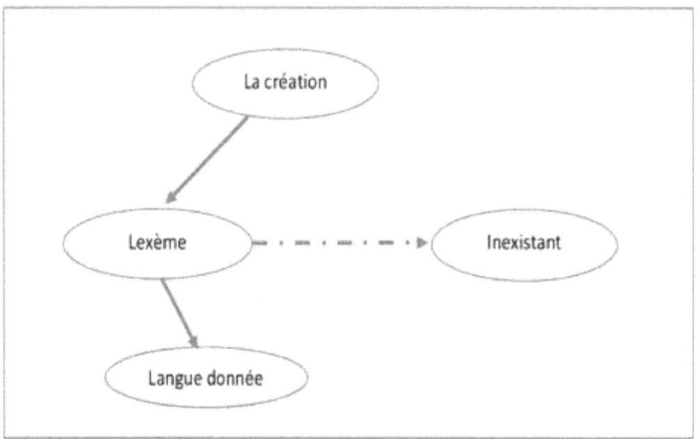

The neology mark *"les " hiraks ""* is already adapted according to the French grammatical system. The lexeme *"les " hiraks ""* is a term of Arabic origin which is transcribed as حراك but the maker of the neology mark *"les " hiraks ""* has transcribed it in French letters, putting it under French grammatical rules (the plural S at the end of the neology mark *"les " hiraks ""* and the article defines les).

In the polyphonic angle, the neological marker *"les "hiraks""* is in perfect harmony with the body text of the Algerian journalistic statement entitled *nous sommes qu'au tout début de la lutte pour la démocratie*. The Algerian journalistic statement *nous sommes qu'au tout début de la lutte pour la démocratie* discreetly contains voices within its internal structure. To deconstruct existing voices, the neology mark *"les " hiraks ""* represents an enunciative responsibility that falls on the back of the enunciator who uttered *"les " hiraks ""*, so the neology mark *"les " hiraks ""* is the voice of a given enunciator. On the other hand, the text of the Algerian journalistic utterance entitled *"We are only at the very beginning of the struggle for democracy"*, which includes the neology mark *"les "hiraks""*, is an enunciative responsibility, strongly attached to the journalist-speaker and representing a second voice of the same journalist-speaker. As a result, the Algerian journalistic statement entitled *nous sommes qu'au tout début de la lutte pour la démocratie* includes a multitude of voices that generate a polyphonic function within the same Algerian journalistic statement entitled *nous sommes qu'au tout début de la lutte pour la démocratie.*

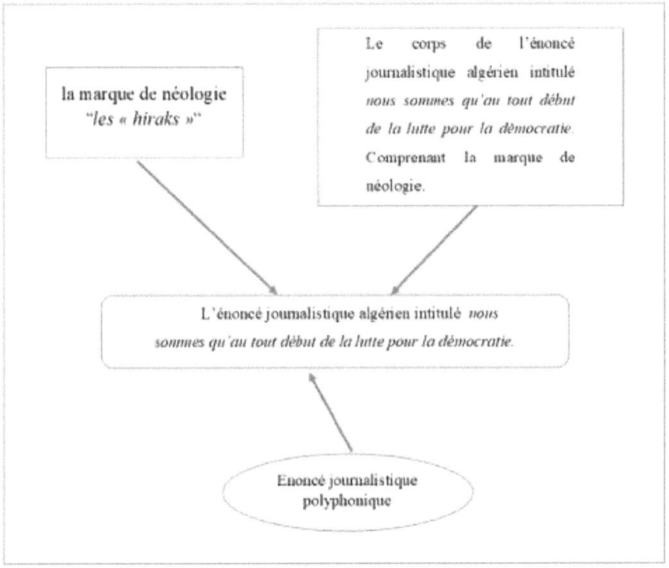

The neology mark "SCAD" refers in an enunciative way to a given enunciator and is the linguistic creation of the latter, "SCAD" is a condensed expression that designates :

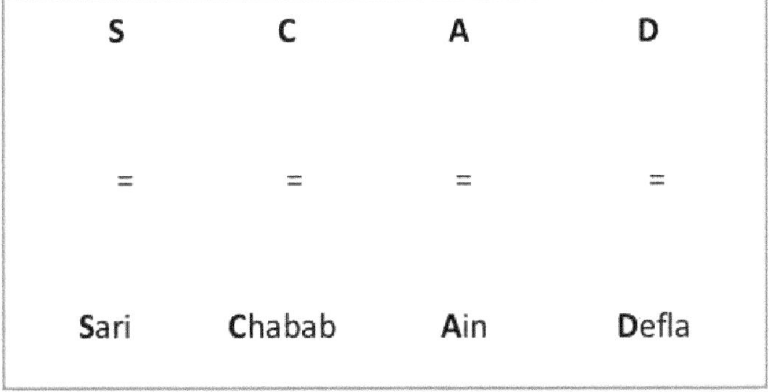

Sari Chabab Ain Defla is an Algerian soccer team based in the wilaya of Ain Defla, Algeria. This "SCAD" brand of neology is in perfect harmony with the body of the Algerian journalistic statement entitled *AFFAIRE IRBBM-SCAD **Une affaire encombrante***, as the enunciator had it subjected to French grammatical standards, in order to produce a lucid and clear semantic concordance for the reader.

Polyphonically, the neology mark "SCAD" represents the voice of the enunciator-creator of the lexeme, who must assume his enunciative responsibility towards it. The structure of the Algerian journalistic statement entitled *AFFAIRE IRBBM-SCAD **Une affaire encombrante*** carrying the neology mark is the voice of the journalist-locuteur, who plays the intermediary role of the reporter between the enunciator-creator and the readership. The Algerian journalistic statement *AFFAIRE IRBBM-SCAD **Une affaire encombrante*** is polyphonic in the sense that it encompasses two polyphonic voices (that of the enunciator-creator and that of the journalist-locuteur).

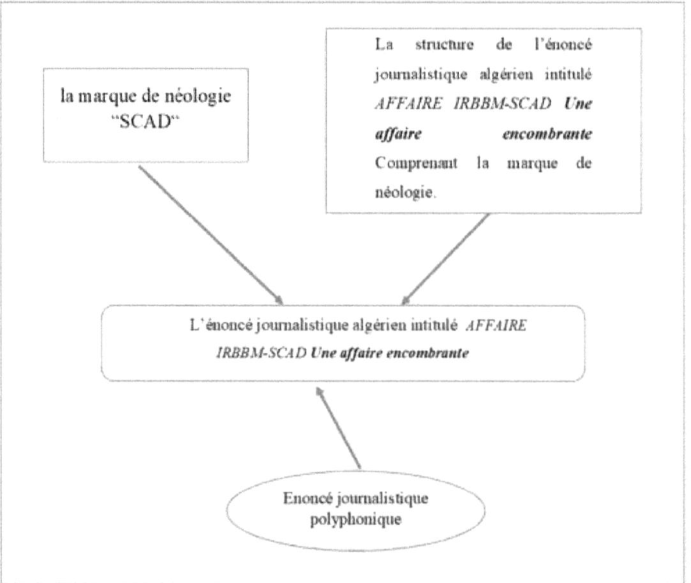

Conclusion

Looking at the historical and linguistic overview of the languages spoken in Algeria, it's clear that there's a real linguistic conflict, since there's a dialect that combines several languages at the same time. While it's true that Algeria is rich in languages spoken within its borders, this has led to a certain amount of resistance between the languages, with each of them trying to take precedence over the other.

When it comes to linguistic polyphony, linguistic diversity in society creates a diversity of discourses, with several discourses in different languages. These discourses are likely to be mediated, which means that each discourse in a given language represents a voice; voices are appropriately linked to their original discourses and to their enunciators, whose enunciative responsibilities they assume towards their products (their discourses=their voices).

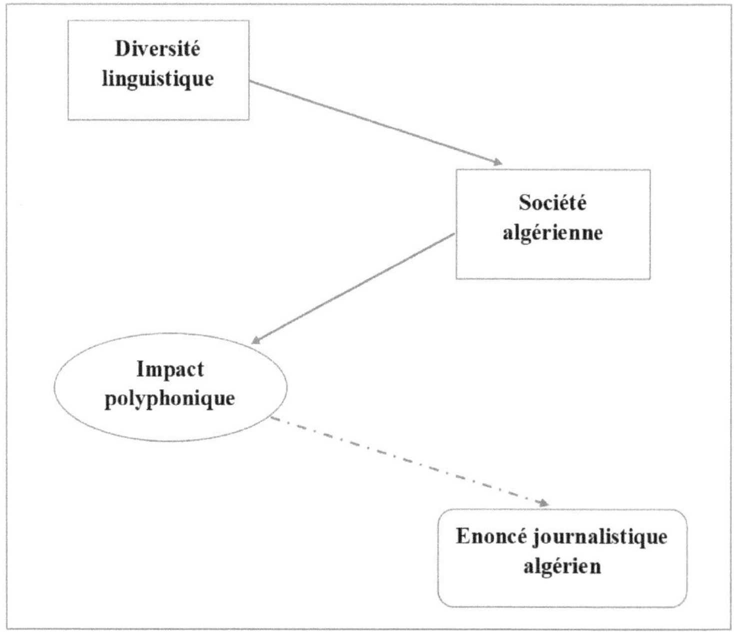

The conflicting situation of linguistic diversity in Algerian society has a strong polyphonic impact on the monophonic or polyphonic situation of the Algerian journalistic statement.

44

In conclusion, the situation of linguistic diversity in Algeria generates a polyphonic function within the Algerian journalistic statement.

Bibliography

Bibliography :

- AUTHIER-REVUZ JACQUELINE. (2020). *La Représentation du Discours Autre Principles for a description*. Degruyter.
- BAKHTIN MIKHAIL. (1984), *"Les genres du discours", in Esthétique de la création verbale*, Paris: Gallimard, pp. 263-308
- BRES J., (2005), *"Le présent de l'indicatif en français : de quelques problèmes, et peut-être de quelques solutions", in Despierres C. and Krazem M. (eds.), Du présent de l'indicatif, Dijon*: Université de Bourgogne, pp. 27-52.
- DUBOIS JEAN ET AL. (1994). *Dictionary of linguistics and language sciences*. Paris: Larousse.
- DUCROT .OSWALD ET AL. (1980). *Les mots du discours.* Paris. Les éditions de minuit.
  - DUCROT, OSWALD. (1984). *Le dire et le dit.* Paris. Minuit.
- GUILBERT LOUIS. (1973). *Théorie du néologisme.* In: Cahiers de l'Association internationale des études francaises, 1973, n°25. pp. 9-29
- GUMPERZ, J-J. (1989): *Engager la conversation*, Paris, Editions de Minuit.
- GUMPERZ, J-J. (1989), *Sociolinguistique interactionnelle. Une approche interprétative*, Paris, L'Harmattan.
- KHAOULA TALEB IBRAHIMI. (2004). Algeria: language coexistence and competition. Open edition journals
- Monir Riadh (2023). Polyphony in journalistic discourse. Heinerich Heine University. Dusseldorf Germany
- NØLKE HENNING. (2017). *Linguistic polyphony: the Scandinavian approach: ScaPoLine*. Brill.

Appendices

CONTRIBUTION

Réappropriation de la Révolution algérienne et /ou de l'indépendance

Par Me Aït-Zaï Nadia

CIDDEF

Le mouvement, le hirak, le sursaut, la Révolution du sourire, comment dénommer ce qui se passe en Algérie ?

Le cinquième mandat est ce qui a fait déborder le vase. Un Président en état d'incapacité de gouverner déclare se présenter de nouveau à la magistrature suprême du pays, alors que quelques mois auparavant, ses fidèles vénéraient son portrait, son cadre, à défaut de l'avoir en face d'eux ou avec eux. En spectateurs de cette mascarade, nous disions notre humiliation en silence, particulièrement lorsque des chefs d'Etat rencontraient le Président en exercice et qui au sortir de l'entrevue exprimaient leur satisfaction de l'avoir vu en bon état d'alacrité, dixit François Hollande. Imaginez la suite, ces personnalités commentant en privé leur rencontre...

Le peuple, ma génération, les partis politiques, spectateurs de cette mascarade, avaient du mal à exprimer leur refus du cinquième mandat pour des raisons multiples. La peur de revivre les années noires de violence qui ont conduit à la perte de plus de 200 000 morts, les calculs politiciens de la classe politique, incapable de s'entendre ou de s'unir autour d'une feuille de route commune et ou aucune femme n'a participé, hormis Louiza Hanoune, la menace brandie par le système, *al'Algérie sera comme*

dans la rue. Les tensions se sont tues, les idéologies identitaires également, même si elles s'expriment en silence, (drapeau berbère). L'Algérie dans sa diversité est redevenue une et indivisible. La femme a trouvé sa place dans ce mouvement communautaire.

A partir du 8 mars, Journée internationale de la femme, des femmes ont manifesté en brandissant des banderoles dont les slogans posaient sur la scène publique des revendications féministes. L'abrogation du Code de la famille et l'application de l'égalité des droits entre les

protectrice, se transforme en détentrice de la morale conservatrice voulue par le Code de la famille. La policière a bien intériorisé ce comportement de dépendance de la femme au groupe, à la communauté. Le communiqué de la police justifie la fouille corporelle des quatre citoyennes, *«comme une mesure qui consiste à ôter tout élément pouvant être utilisé par les personnes interpellées contre elles-mêmes ou contre autrui».* Le communiqué est maladroit, surtout lorsqu'il évoque le *«contre elles -mêmes»,* les filles ont manifesté, ce n'était pas des folies en crise ou des suicidaires. Le message était-il de nous faire comprendre que les femmes n'ont pas de raison ? Idée fortement ancrée dans les consciences et appliquée, puisque nous ne pouvons pas témoigner dans des actes officiels. Il nous est interdit de le faire, et ce, sans base légale, interdiction appliquée dès la promulgation du Code de la famille et surtout en référence à la tradition musulmane.

Peuvent-elles, peut-on être des citoyennes, des individus quand leur liberté, notre liberté est confisquée, contrôlée, hypothéquée et subordonnée à l'autorité du père, du frère, du mari ? Il ne s'agit pas de clamer ce droit constitutionnel, il faut le rendre effectif, l'exercer, ne pas avoir peur de le faire. Des étudiantes en conclave à Constantine, pour un débat sur le prolongement de la grève, ont soulevé les interdits familiaux auxquels elles sont confrontées, retour au domicile pour celles qui habitent hors de la wilaya d'étude si elles n'ont pas cours. Elles sont conscientes, réfléchissent, il faut qu'elles définissent elles-mêmes ce qu'elles veulent être.

ENTRETIEN

MADJID BENCHIKH. *Professeur émérite à l'Université de Cergy-Pontoise*

«Nous ne sommes qu'au tout début

Le professeur Madjid Benchikh dresse, dans cet entretien, un bilan du «soulèvement populaire» comme il l'appelle, après trois mois de mobilisation ininterrompue. L'auteur de *Algérie : un système politique militarisé* analyse également le rôle du commandement militaire dans la gestion de l'après-Bouteflika. Le juriste estime que sortir de l'ordre constitutionnel actuel ne va pas propulser le pays dans le chaos mais, au contraire, «ouvrir la voie à des institutions de transition démocratique susceptibles de redonner espoir au peuple». Il évoque, par ailleurs, son rôle au sein de la société civile pour l'élaboration d'un plan de transition consensuel, qui pourrait constituer une alternative sérieuse à la tenue d'une élection présidentielle condamnée à l'échec, et jeter les fondements de la nouvelle République.

Entretien réalisé par
Mustapha Benfodil

Nous en sommes à plus de trois mois de mobilisation populaire pour un changement radical du système politique. Quel bilan faites-vous du hirak, professeur ?

La mobilisation populaire a obtenu des victoires d'étape importantes qui doivent être soulignées. Le hirak est devenu rapidement un véritable soulèvement populaire qui montre un peuple debout, qui affirme sa dignité et

PHOTO : SAMI K.

d'avancer que de reculer. La mobilisation doit continuer, y compris durant la transition démocratique. Elle doit garder sa force, sa détermination et surtout son intelligence pour répondre de façon appropriée aux manœuvres des tenants du système et tenir sur une longue période. Les derniers vendredis ont montré que, malgré le Ramadhan, le peuple sait faire la part des manœuvres et des luttes de clans relatives par exemple aux arrestations de ceux qui ont perdu le pouvoir. Le peuple montre qu'il reste concentré sur l'essentiel : il veut résolument obtenir le changement du système. C'est le

«RENONCER À L'ORGANISATION DE L'ÉLECTION DU 4 JUILLET C'EST, NON PAS AVANCER VERS LE CHAOS, MAIS, AU CONTRAIRE, ENGAGER UN PROCESSUS POLITIQUE QUI PERMETTRAIT DE

décideurs de se rapprocher de ceux qui luttent pour une transition démocratique et pas seulement de chanter la beauté du hirak pour ensuite le poignarder dans le dos. Ce n'est pas intelligent, ni même honnête. Cela ne mène à rien de constructif.

Tout bien considéré, il n'y a donc aucun danger à annuler les élections. Cela va diminuer la pression, et, du coup, permettra d'engager un dialogue avec la société civile, avec les syndicats autonomes, avec les personnalités indépendantes qui aspirent à la construction de la démocratie et peuvent, dès lors, apporter leur contribution à cette construction. Moi, je suis sûr que ce n'est pas se projeter dans le vide que d'aller dans cette direction mais, au contraire, s'engager dans la voie de la construction d'une nouvelle République qui reposera sur l'adhésion des populations. Cette adhésion transformera la nature de l'Etat sur les plans politique et juridique. Le peuple veut que les services publics fonctionnent bien, que les chemins de fer fonctionnent bien, que les transports fonctionnent bien, que la poste fonctionne bien, que la police accomplisse convenablement son travail, que la justice soit indépendante et «juste»… C'est cela l'Etat. Ce sont là les services publics principaux qui forment la colonne vertébrale de l'Etat. Et le peuple veut les protéger comme il le montre chaque vendredi. Par conséquent, si on avance dans la réalisation des aspirations de la population, portées par le soulèvement populaire, nous irons vers un Etat plus fort, plus solide que jamais. J'appelle le commandement militaire à réfléchir aux effets bénéfiques qui résultent de la confiance du peuple dans son Etat pour l'accomplissement des missions traditionnelles de toute armée moderne. Je l'appelle à engager revendique les droits humains et les libertés démocratiques. C'est un véritable soulèvement parce que le peuple, en se mettant debout, désigne clairement son objectif : abattre le système autoritaire qui l'étouffait. Debout, il regarde non seulement devant lui mais aussi vers l'horizon. Il a dès lors des perspectives que ne définissent pas toujours les «hiraks» : il revendique un Etat démocratique. C'est un soulèvement populaire qui peut demain devenir une véritable révolution.

Le soulèvement a forcé Bouteflika à renoncer au 5ᵉ mandat, puis à la prolongation du 4ᵉ. Il l'a forcé à la démission. Il a même forcé le commandement militaire qui a, jusque-là, soutenu très clairement le 5ᵉ mandat, à intervenir pour demander le départ de Bouteflika. La mobilisation populaire a donc bouleversé les données de la scène politique. Elle a perturbé le système politique autoritaire sans cependant le terrasser. Il convient maintenant de se mobiliser pour obtenir le plus important et le plus difficile qui est le changement radical du système. Continuer à se mobiliser doit être le maître-mot pour aller vers une transition démocratique. Un peu comme le Romain Scipion l'Africain qui répétait toujours qu'il fallait détruire Carthage pour se rendre maître de la Méditerranée, le soulèvement populaire doit se mobiliser encore et toujours pour «dégager» le système autoritaire.

Ce soulèvement est ainsi porteur d'espoir. On peut déjà penser à plusieurs conséquences politiques pour l'avenir. Je pense notamment que les gouvernants auront désormais, quoi qu'il arrive, des difficultés à soumettre les populations. Ils ne pourront pas mettre en prison une grande partie de la jeunesse. Les partis politiques actuels seront probablement balayés, d'autant qu'ils sont pour la plupart très peu représentatifs. Le vieux doyen que je suis, pour reprendre le mot d'un journaliste, considère que ce soulèvement populaire obligera quiconque voudra gouverner à donner un vrai «coup de jeune» aux institutions politiques, économiques et sociales. A tous points de vue, ce soulèvement marque un tournant dans la vie politique dans notre pays. Le commandement militaire et les gouvernants devront en tenir compte…

Il reste cependant beaucoup à faire. Nous des peuples qui se mettent debout, de concentrer leurs énergies sur les objectifs essentiels.

Tous les vendredis, les Algériens expriment clairement leur rejet de l'élection présidentielle du 4 juillet. De son côté, M. Gaïd Salah nous signifie qu'en dehors du scrutin, c'est le chaos, en laissant entendre qu'une situation de vide constitutionnel pourrait être fatale pour notre pays. Objectivement, quelles pourraient être les conséquences d'un deuxième report de l'élection présidentielle ?

Renoncer à l'organisation des élections du 4 juillet c'est, non pas avancer vers le chaos, mais, au contraire, engager un processus politique qui permettrait de quitter un ordre constitutionnel autoritaire et sans légitimité populaire pour construire un ordre qui répond aux aspirations de notre peuple et notamment de sa jeunesse. Renoncer à l'élection du 4 juillet signifierait que l'état-major se résout à abandonner des positions qui le mènent droit dans le mur. On est donc loin de l'idée selon laquelle se dégager de cette application catastrophique de l'article 102, c'est entrer dans un vide juridique ou une situation de chaos dans l'organisation de l'Etat. J'entends même des juristes qui ont préconisé le recours à l'article 102 reconnaître maintenant l'impasse à laquelle il conduit.

Aujourd'hui, le vide est représenté par les institutions qui reposent sur la Constitution actuelle. Cette Constitution et ses institutions ont objectivement couvert les dérives du système politique et des gouvernants vers la corruption et l'arbitraire, avec l'appui de toutes les forces qui ont construit le système et l'intervention des oligarchies qui en profitent. C'est là un système bloqué devenu dangereux pour l'essor du peuple algérien et pour le développement de l'Algérie. Actuellement, ces institutions ne se réunissent même pas. Elles sont inutiles. Il est urgent de les abandonner. Qui peut croire qu'une Assemblée nationale depuis longtemps discréditée et mal élue et un Sénat qui est une insulte à la démocratie, notamment par l'existence de son tiers présidentiel, sont des institutions parlementaires dignes de ce nom. Le peuple les associe aux quotas de députés et de sénateurs fixés par les

désignant les sacs noirs dans lesquels les nouveaux riches distribuent l'argent destiné à pervertir les élections et l'élaboration des décisions. Tout cela milite pour la dissolution immédiate de ces institutions pour ouvrir la voie à des institutions de transition démocratique susceptibles de redonner espoir au peuple. C'est cela «accompagner» effectivement, et non en paroles, les revendications du soulèvement populaire. Continuer à vouloir organiser ces élections contre la volonté mille fois exprimée par des dizaines de millions d'Algériens et maintenir Bensalah, Bedoui, le Parlement et le Conseil constitutionnel, indique un attachement au système actuel sur lequel il est légitime de s'interroger. Surtout lorsque de tels discours viennent de ceux qui ont soutenu le 4ᵉ et le 5ᵉ mandats. Les Algériens qui manifestent savent bien comment a été édifié le système et qui en profite. C'est tout cela qui fait que les discours de Gaïd Salah sont hors sol et nient la réalité. Le commandement serait-il obnubilé par les avantages qu'il tire d'un système qu'il a toujours dominé ? Il risquerait alors de retomber dans les dérives du Président déchu.

On aboutit ainsi forcément à des analyses politiques faibles ou inconsistantes. Mais en même temps, tout cela est évidemment dommageable pour notre pays. Il est même dangereux, pour aujourd'hui et pour l'avenir, de ne pas avoir des décideurs capables de montrer une vision, sur la base d'une analyse politique sérieuse, basée sur l'histoire du système politique et soucieuse de comprendre les raisons de la mobilisation populaire contre le système

système politique qui nous a conduit aux dérives que l'on sait

Vous avez toujours insisté sur le fait que le régime politique en Algérie est une «démocratie de façade», et qu'il y a une «permanence de l'emprise de l'armée sur le système politique». Cette question est d'ailleurs au cœur de votre livre Algérie : un système politique militarisé. Quelle lecture faites-vous du rôle de l'armée dans la gestion de l'après-Bouteflika ? Gaïd Salah peut-il lâcher du lest, selon vous, et accepter d'aller vers une véritable transition démocratique, lui qui semble très attaché à la légalité constitutionnelle en rejetant toute solution «politique» ?

Le passage à une démocratie implique que le commandement militaire ne sera plus au centre du pouvoir. Cela signifie la fin d'un système qui organise son emprise sur les principales institutions et sur la vie politique. Le commandement militaire organise cette emprise tout en se mettant à l'arrière-plan du système politique, sans gouverner au-devant de la scène, c'est-à-dire apparemment sans gérer lui-même les ministères et les entreprises. Et ce fonctionnement date depuis l'indépendance du pays. A partir de 1989, on a un texte constitutionnel de type démocratique, mais le maintien de l'emprise du commandement militaire sur la vie politique ne permet d'aboutir qu'à une démocratie de façade.

L'emprise s'exerce d'abord par le fait que c'est toujours le commandement militaire qui choisit la pièce maîtresse du système, c'est-à-dire le chef de l'Etat, puis le fait élire avec des élections truquées. Tous les chefs de l'Etat en Algérie ont été désignés de cette manière. C'est le commandement militaire qui a ramené Ben Bella, qui a désigné Chadli, Boudiaf, Liamine Zeroual, et aussi celui qui vient de partir (Bouteflika, ndlr)… On est d'emblée au cœur de la militarisation du système.

Mais il y a plus et peut-être encore plus important. Le commandement militaire a mis à sa disposition, pour tout ce qui concerne l'élaboration des grandes décisions politiques, la Sécurité militaire, devenue par la suite DRS. Le DRS constitue à ce titre l'organisme qui s'occupe «du politique», au service du d'entre les militants engagés, ou la menace tout court de vous priver de votre liberté non sans pour autant vous avoir au passage traité de traître à l'Etat algérien, car les décideurs se sont sentis dépositaires du nationalisme et de la distribution des bons points à ceux qui les suivent.

Mais voilà, à la grande surprise de tous, des jeunes se sont réappropriés l'espace public longtemps confisqué par le pouvoir, faisant dire à Benjamin Stora : *«Incontestablement, il s'agit d'une page d'histoire très importante de l'Algérie contemporaine qui nous renvoie aux grandes fêtes de l'été 62, les fêtes de l'indépendance.»* Il ajoute : *«Il ne faut pas oublier que la Révolution algérienne est le fait des jeunes.»*

Une jeunesse que l'on croyait perdue, démobilisée, dépolitisée s'est avérée être une jeunesse créative, innovante, drôle, festive, ayant du ressort. Il n'y a qu'un seul 5, c'est celui de Chanel, a écrit un jeune sur sa pancarte.

Deuxième Révolution, deuxième République, continuité de la Révolution algérienne, ou alors simplement réappropriation de l'indépendance ?

Leurs mots d'ordre, hormis le refus du 5e mandat, le départ du système, des tenants du pouvoir, le départ des trois B, c'est aussi et surtout l'Etat de droit, la liberté, l'abolition des privilèges, la justice sociale, la redistribution des richesses du pays, l'égalité des chances. Grâce à eux, nous nous sentons délestés d'un poids trop longtemps porté sur nos épaules, les courbant et redressées grâce à leur énergie. Nous avons retrouvé la parole et recouvré notre dignité.

Cette jeunesse n'est-elle composée que de jeunes hommes ? Non, les femmes, tous âges confondus, ont massivement rejoint, investi, ce mouvement de révolte, particulièrement les étudiantes et les jeunes militantes du mouvement associatif, ainsi que les femmes des corporations professionnelles, avocats, médecins et autres. Ce qui donne la force au mouvement et son caractère pacifique, c'est la présence des personnes âgées, femmes et hommes, des familles, des bébés et enfants. Les Algériens, de toutes conditions sociales, se côtoient, se parlent et s'initient au vivre-ensemble en se découvrant et en s'entraidant hommes et les femmes. A Béjaïa, un collectif de femmes a demandé l'abrogation de la clause de pardon relative à l'article 341 bis du Code pénal promulgué dans le cadre de la loi contre les violences faites aux femmes. Oran et les autres wilayas n'étaient pas en reste de la célébration de cette journée redevenue revendicative et non festive.

Le vendredi 29 mars à Alger, des hommes ont agressé, verbalement et physiquement, le groupe du collectif de femmes algériennes pour un changement vers l'égalité, qui manifestait à Alger-Centre, debout sur le trottoir, dans un carré appelé carré féministe, près de la fac centrale.

Ce n'est pas le moment. Vous divisez le mouvement, un seul mot d'ordre, «Non au cinquième mandat», criaient les hommes, je dirais les meneurs. Les banderoles furent arrachées, des femmes agressées verbalement, frappées et arrosées d'eau pour les disperser. Silmia, Silmia, criaient les femmes agressées, terme utilisé par l'ensemble des manifestants pour donner un caractère pacifique au mouvement et ne pas répondre aux provocations des services de sécurité, sauf que dans cette situation, les policiers présents sollicités ne sont pas intervenus.

«Ce n'est pas le moment» est aussi brandi par des femmes, qui souhaiteraient voir partir le système d'abord et instaurer l'Etat de droit ou l'égalité s'instaurerait naturellement. Cela nous rappelle les discours politiques des années 1976, où il était écrit : «La femme algérienne en participant au développement économique du pays accéderait à l'égalité», Mohamed Harbi répliquait : «C'est un euphémisme de croire, de penser que parce que la femme algérienne a participé à la libération du pays elle aurait acquis sa liberté.»

Une moudjahida, Baya Hocine, dans le même sillage, déclare : *«Nous avons franchi les digues de la tradition en rejoignant les maquis, en 1962, les digues se sont refermées sur nous.»*

Est-il de tradition de voir les femmes défiler, participer à des mouvements, oui bien entendu, il faut se souvenir des années, 1962, 1990, 1995, 2000, pour se faire une idée de l'engagement politique des femmes, qui gardent en mémoire et comme modèles les moudjahidate, à l'instar de Hassiba Ben Bouali, morte à 17 ans, de Djamila Bouazza, décédée, de Djamila Bouhired, de Louizette Ighil Ahriz, qui se sont

CELUI DE CHANEL, A ÉCRIT UN JEUNE SUR SA PANCARTE. DEUXIÈME RÉVOLUTION, DEUXIÈME RÉPUBLIQUE, CONTINUITÉ DE LA RÉVOLUTION ALGÉRIENNE, OU ALORS SIMPLEMENT RÉAPPROPRIATION DE L'INDÉPENDANCE ?

mêlées aux manifestants, rappelant au passage la confiscation de l'indépendance de l'Algérie.

Le pays est en péril, je le défends, je n'attends pas la permission de mes tuteurs, je brave l'interdit, disaient les moudjahidate et militantes. A ces périodes et cela ressemble étrangement à aujourd'hui, lorsqu'on mettait en avant les droits des femmes, l'abrogation du Code de la famille, on nous rétorquait : *«Ce n'est pas le moment.»* Ce n'est jamais le moment de penser, de réfléchir la citoyenneté de la femme dans l'espace privé au même titre que celle de l'homme, il faut se taire, on serait tenté d'adopter la maxime : «Cachez ce sein que je ne saurais voir.»

Liberté, scandent les jeunes hommes et jeunes femmes, Comment la réfléchissent-ils ? Si cette liberté, cette égalité n'est pas réfléchie dans le cadre d'un choix rapide d'un projet de société, elle risque, comme à l'indépendance en 1962 et durant les années de braise en 1995 de devenir éphémère, transparente, être comme dit l'adage arabe : «Hibra ala Ouarek.»

Liberté de manifester dans les rues les jours de semaine, les filles l'ont appris à leurs dépens. Elles ont été arrêtées, conduites au commissariat et mises à nu pour une fouille, alors que les hommes qui ont été arrêtés ne l'ont pas été. La fouille fut-elle délibérée ? Fût-elle faite par une femme policière pour les humilier, pour leur rappeler leur condition de femme, pour annihiler leur liberté ? Si oui, c'est alors une liberté qui appartiendrait en prolongement de la famille à l'institution qui, au lieu d'être de février 2019, consacrée aux jeunes (8,76 millions de jeunes ont moins de 25 ans pour une population de 42 millions d'habitants), a révélé que *«très majoritairement, la jeunesse algérienne approuve la séparation de la religion et de l'Etat»*. Deux tiers des jeunes interrogés sont contre l'interférence du religieux dans la vie politique. La répartition des réponses par genre donne 63% pour les filles, 67% pour les garçons.

L'enquête révèle que très peu de jeunes accordent confiance en leurs institutions et la politique partisane peu attractive, ce qui explique les exclusions des partis politiques du mouvement de manifestation et les mots d'ordre contre le système.

Seront-ils entendus, avec qui négocier, avec qui dialoguer, leurs demandes se transformeront-elles en un projet de société ? quelqu'un a dit que tous les mots d'ordre réunis dans ce mouvement peuvent être compilés et transformés en Constitution.

Respect des droits individuels, liberté, égalité en droits entre les hommes et les femmes, séparation des trois pouvoirs, transparence, état de droit, justice sociale, distribution équitable des richesses, souveraineté du peuple.

Le mouvement ne veut pas se doter de leader de peur de voir celui-ci être phagocité, les jeunes filles et garçons sont à l'affût, selon leur propos, de toute personne qui veut surfer sur la vague. Personne n'ose dire, je représente le mouvement. Ils doivent tous partir, «Itnahaou Gaâ», scandent les manifestants

A la douzième sortie, les demandes sont les mêmes, départ du système, des propositions de sortie de crise sont proposées par différents groupes, mais les dirigeants, jusque-là, restent sourds aux sollicitations des citoyens.

La solution constitutionnelle est dépassée, il reste la solution politique, la négociation d'où ne doivent pas être exclus les jeunes et les femmes.

Pour les femmes, la résolution 13/25 l'exige.

La résolution impose aux différentes parties en conflit de respecter les droits des femmes et de soutenir leur participation aux négociations de paix et à la reconstruction post-conflit.

A. Z. N.

MAK and MCB calm down

To commemorate the double anniversary of the Berber Spring and the Black Spring, several hundred citizens marched through the streets of Bouira, chanting anti-government slogans and demanding the officialization of Tamazight. From the early hours of the morning, buses streamed towards the starting point of this march called by the MCB and the MAK. At around 9 a.m., a dozen young people were stopped by police as they prepared to unfurl banners in front of the Akli-Mohand-Oulhadj university. Following talks between police and MCB militants, the young people were released a few minutes later. The first square of marchers, made up of MAK militants, took to the boulevard leading up to the wilaya headquarters. "Pouvoir assassin", "Ulac smah ulac", "Azul fellawen", "Tubiret dImazighen" were chanted at the top of their voices along the way. The second square, made up of MCB militants, followed the same route, but not chanting the same slogans. Arriving in front of the wilaya headquarters, where police were deployed, the two squares regrouped before moving on to the esplanade of the Maison de la Culture Ali-Zaâmoum. Bellal Nouredine, an MCB supporter and one of the march's initiators, improvised a speech on the spot. "This year, we're celebrating the 34th anniversary of the Amazigh Spring in a very special context. We're here today to demand recognition of the Amazigh identity and language, and respect for democratic freedoms. We are also speaking out against impunity for those responsible for the 2001 Black Spring massacres, and we wish to lend our support and reaffirm our solidarity with the Mozabites." The young MAK demonstrators tried to take the floor to explain their point of view, as they do every April 20th, by attacking the stele representing Emir Abdelkader erected in the heart of the town of Bouira. However, they were quickly brought to their senses by the wisdom of the MCB militants, who emphasized the peaceful nature of the action. The marchers dispersed peacefully and no incidents were reported. April 13, 2019

The case of IRB Bou Medfaa Ŕ SC Aïn Defla (centre-west group of the inter-regional league) continues to be the talk of the town more than a month after the incidents that led to the final stoppage of the game, when the score was 1-1. As a reminder, in the first instance, the LIRF Disciplinary Committee awarded the match to the visiting team.
match to the visiting team (SCAD), following reports from the match officials, referee Ibrir and the two delegates, Hemani and Douib. IRB Bou Medfaa lodged an appeal, after which the Federal Appeals Commission decided to reschedule the match. The two contradictory decisions handed down by the LIRF Disciplinary Committee and then the Appeals Committee will require arbitration by the Federal Board, which is due to rule on the matter tomorrow, Monday. There are several contradictory versions and too many grey areas in this case.
case. Starting with the real reasons behind the presence on the pitch of the visiting team's supporters (SCAD). According to a document submitted by the IRBBM, i.e. the report from the Bou Medfaa gendarmerie, "the visiting team's supporters invaded the pitch under the pretext that stones had been thrown at them". This version is contradicted by the report from the same institution, namely the Aïn Defla command, which states: "SCAD supporters entered the pitch under the pressure of stone-throwing." There is a difference in the use of the terms "under pretext" and "under pressure".

I want morebooks!

Buy your books fast and straightforward online - at one of world's fastest growing online book stores! Environmentally sound due to Print-on-Demand technologies.

Buy your books online at
www.morebooks.shop

Kaufen Sie Ihre Bücher schnell und unkompliziert online – auf einer der am schnellsten wachsenden Buchhandelsplattformen weltweit! Dank Print-On-Demand umwelt- und ressourcenschonend produziert.

Bücher schneller online kaufen
www.morebooks.shop

Printed by Books on Demand GmbH, Norderstedt / Germany